77 Date Night Ideas That Will Enhance Your Relationship or Marriage.

Date Night

"He brought me to the banqueting house, and his banner over me was love." Song of Solomon 2:4

Dexter & Petula Jones

UWriteIt Publishing Company
Goldsboro, NC USA
www.uwriteitpublishingcompany.com
www.soulmateorjustadate.com

Date Night by Dexter & Petula Jones
Copyright © 2011 by Dexter & Petula Jones
ALL RIGHTS RESERVED

ISBN: **ISBN-13:978-0615537443 (UWriteIt Publishing Company)**
ISBN-10:0615537448

First Printing September – 2011

NO PART OF THIS BOOK MAY BE REPRODUCED IN ANY FORM, BY PHOTOCOPYING OR BY ANY ELECTRONIC OR MECHANICAL MEANS, INCLUDING INFORMATION STORAGE OR RETRIEVAL SYSTEMS, WITHOUT PERMISSION IN WRITING FROM THE COPYRIGHT OWNER/AUTHOR

Unless otherwise indicated, Scripture quotations in this book are from the King James Version of the Bible.

This publication is designed to provide information in regard to the subject matter covered. It is published with the understanding that the authors are not engaged in rendering legal counsel or other professional services. If legal advice or other professional advice is required, the services of a professional person should be sought.

Printed in the U.S.A.

Dedication

We dedicate this book to our Lord and Savior Jesus Christ who is the head of our lives. We dedicate this book to our heavenly Father for blessing us with a marriage that is truly ordained from heaven, a God given relationship between Soul Mates. We dedicate this book to our children Brandon and Jasmine, you are the seeds of the righteous, and therefore we know that God shall bless you both in life with the mate of your souls.

Table of Contents

Introduction

Date Night

Together

Ideas for Married Couples Only

Ideas for Couples in Relationships

God's Ideal Relationship

Walk In Love

Introduction

As we behold the divorce rate in our land today with one out of every two marriages ending in divorce, truly there is a problem going on. Not only have individuals not met their Soul Mates in life but even the ones that have have not gone on to realize that a marriage takes work. The success or failure of every marriage begins in the relationship stage, individuals are missing it in the dating stage and divorces are merely the inevitable conclusion of such actions. Men and women have failed to realize that there are needs which are essential for both parties involved and if these needs are not met then consequences will follow. Just having a relationship or marriage is not enough there must be time spent **together** in order to create a bond of affection and unity. Most couples have omitted this essential key of togetherness and they wonder why their relationship or marriage is suffering.

If you want to have relationship success you must begin to incorporate togetherness in your relationship or marriage. One of the ways to do this is through a Date Night and we have listed 77 Date Night Ideas that will enhance your relationship or marriage. The key word is together which is defined as having contact or union with each other.

If you want a relationship or marriage like you have never had then you must begin to do something that you have never done. You can't expect something different following the same pattern. As a couple you must begin to incorporate within your life a date night. The two of you must pick a night that you can get together for the mere pleasure of being together and enjoying each other's company. Here are 77 new ways of doing things that will bring about a change in your relationship or married life.

1

Date Night

"I am my beloved's and his desire is toward me." Song of Solomon 7:10

Date Night is not a new concept although it may be new to many. Date Night consist of a couple coming together in order to spend time in the presence and company of their spouse or significant other. Date Night is a lost art in many relationships today and as result we have many relationships that are symbolically speaking going down the drain. Many of these relationships could be savaged by doing simple things; however when mankind refuses to learn these simple things their relationship is often destroyed.

Do you remember the first time the two of you met or became acquainted with each other? Whether you met through cyberspace online or in person there was an immediate attraction or something toward each other. You could hardly wait for the next meeting when the two of you would get together and spend time in each other's presence.

Together was the key word of your acquaintance and the more time you spent together with this person the more time you wanted to spend with them.

It was as if time had stood still and your heart leaped with joy just at the mention of their name. The two of you knew that you had something special and just being acquaintances was not enough, you wanted to take it to the next step, serious dating and commitment with each other. The two of you even dangled in the dating stage that maybe this could be your soul mate.

With this individual you felt like you had great compatibility and a great spiritual, soul (mental), and physical attraction to. Someone when you look at it's like you're looking at a mirror image of yourself and to this person you wanted to make a lifetime commitment with. And the feeling was mutual with both of you. When you met this person it was like it had the touch of divine grace, mercy and amazement upon it and on earth nothing was more precious in life.

You Imagined…………………

- Having someone to love you as much as you loved him or her.
- Having someone to treat you with the utmost respect, love and kindness.
- Having someone that wouldn't take you for granted but would love and cherish you.
- Having someone that understood you.
- Having someone that allowed you to be you.

- Having someone that was a good communicator to you.
- Having someone that made you feel like you're the greatest person on earth, HIS QUEEN.
- Having someone that made you feel like you're the greatest person on earth, HER KING.
- Having someone that enjoyed being in your presence.
- Having someone that brought out the best in you.

You knew that you had found your good thing and it was just a matter of time before you popped the big question. Everything seemed so right and the thoughts of a life of bliss and total fulfillment were just around the corner. So the two of you took the big step and could only see good days ahead, but somewhere along the way the bliss faded and good days turned into bad days for some and days of just enduring for others.

Some did not take the big step but just decided to continue in this blissful relationship with expectations of a joyous relationship life together. There were many positive factors that stood out such as the two of you looked for ways to maintain interest.

You had trust, commitment, caring and the other positive factors that make up a good relationship. However, somewhere along the way that joyous relationship turned into a relationship of barely getting alone.

Gone were the days of anticipation of seeing each other and looking forward to spending time together. Somewhere along the way the relationship begin to deteriorate and fade and the once blissful couple (either one or both) now beings to see the relationship as less desirable than it once was.

Many negatives begin to enter the relationship and the positive factors that once held the relationship in heavenly bliss now seems to be obsolete. No longer did the two of you invest time and put forth the necessary effort in the relationship like you did when you first started dating. When you first started out you were patient with each other, you worked to improve the relationship and you did the most important thing, you spent time together. You went out on dates even if it was just a ride to the store with each other. Here is a list of some of the things you did in the beginning:

- You went out to get ice cream together.
- You went to the movies together.
- You went to church together.
- You took road trips together.

- You went on a picnic together.
- You went hiking together.
- You went out to dinner together.
- You went hunting together.
- You went bike riding together.
- You stayed in and watched a movie together and ate popcorn.
- You went out for pizza.
- You cooked a meal together.
- You went with each other to get their hair done or cut.
- You exercised together.
- All the family went out and made an evening of it and had a joyous event.
- You went shopping together and treated each other.
- You had a romantic dinner at your favorite restaurant.
- You bought flowers and candy and teddy bears just because.
- You spent time reading a good book together.
- You just enjoyed each other's presence.

So what happened to cause the rift in the marriage or the relationship? One of the things that happened is the two of you stopped dating. Some begin to take each other for granted and others did not see the necessity of continuing to do what it took in the beginning to keep it fresh and fulfilling.

Today, I want to encourage you that if the two of you are still together in spite of the deterioration of the marriage or relationship it can be saved if the two of you still want to save it. Even if only one of you wants to save it there is still hope if you're willing to put in the necessary time to bring back the spark.

If the two of you or either of you is Christians you stand a great chance of God blessing this union and turning it around. Prayer is still the greatest weapon in the world for any situation and faith can still unlock any door. So begin to pray for your marriage or relationship and put it before God and ask him to help and strengthen you for the task ahead. If you're in a relationship only, put it before the Lord and ask God is this relationship of him or is it a relationship that you got in without truly acknowledging him. A relationship is not as weighty as a marriage because a relationship has no legal strings attached and you can more easily get out of it and count your losses.

Another thing about a relationship is that if there are too many negatives in the relationship and it has constantly been an on again off again relationship, you already have your answer. Just receive it. If you still can't receive it well here is some cold hard truth?

On again / off again relationships are designed to turn your emotional world upside down. We all at one time or another have been in a relationship where the connection has been on at time and off at times. The off times of the relationship were times that brought about a rift in the connection. No relationships are going to be without its challenges and disagreements. It's ok to disagree but mature individuals learn how to disagree without being disagreeable. Immature individuals disagree and either calls it quits or part ways with much animosity and hostility.

The truth about on again / off again relationships is that they create much frustration and a whirlwind of emotional chaos and confusion. On again/off again relationships are designed to turn your emotional world upside down and keep you in a state of disillusionment and opposition that can even turn into hatred.

On again / off again relationships rarely end up a happy relationship and the two parties end up with a broken heart and broken promises. Now let's look at some hard cold truths:

- Somebody in the relationship doesn't want to really be with the other.
- The reason that your relationship is on again / off again is because the interest level that you have in each other is not high enough to create a true bond. One of your interest levels is high and the other is low.
- Things are good for a while a month or so and then you are right back where you started.
- You think you have a bond because of the longevity of your relationship but it's a farce. a foolish show, a mockery and a ridiculous sham. (I wish I could tell you this is going to get more to your liking but it's not.)
- The reason you continue in this foolishness is because you are opposites and you believe the lie that opposites are good for each other. Well all opposites do is attract each other but they have no power to make good on it or produce substance out of the relationship.
- The two of you are simply pretending to have a good relationship but deep down you know you want out because it's empty, dead, void and keep you on an emotional roller coaster ride.
- Your on again / off again relationship is nothing but a yo-yo connection and it has already created years of torture for you.

- It's not a match made in heaven but a match made in hell and if it doesn't literally send you to hell it will keep you living in hell on earth.

- Somebody is simply stringing the other along, besides they know you will be back because you have already been back 20 plus times what does one more time matter. Then this one more time turns into one more time, then one more time, then one more time etc... How many times are you going to split up before you wake up and smell the coffee as they say? Let go and get on with your life. God did not create you for this mess.

The scripture says, *"The thief (the devil) cometh but to steal, and to kill, and to destroy: I am come (Jesus) that they (you) might have life, and that they (you) might have it more abundantly."* John 10:10 The devil is using your on again / off again relationship to steal the joy out of your life, to kill off your emotional well-being and to eventually destroy your life and your pursuit of happiness. Jesus has come to give you joy, the life of God and to give it to you in such an abundance that you can spend your days living life to the fullest in every aspect of your life.

There is a great relationship and a great person out there for you, but you must decide if you will continue with your on again / off again relationship for another year or will you make this your year of change. If you don't have enough fortitude or mental and emotional strength to do it for yourself then do it for your children (if children are involved in your life) or your family who is tired of seeing your life in turmoil and difficulty.

For those that are married or in a good relationship but it has lost its spark, you must get back to dating once again. Remember, the key word during your dating stage was together, make that your key word again and watch what happens. Don't just sit back and be passive, take action and become an active participant. Prayer is great but faith without works is dead, being alone. Do your part to make this union once again a blissful and joyous marriage or relationship.

2

Together

"For this cause shall a man leave his father and mother, and shall be joined unto his wife, and they two shall be one flesh." Ephesians 5:31

    The word together is such a powerful word that I believe that we have omitted the power that is inherited in this one word. The word together is defined as being jointly, as one, mutually, in concert, collectively, concurrently, in sync, organized, unruffled and composed. The word together carries such weight that the only time this word is null and void is when it has no necessity of being with another. Then the word alone comes into play when means being unaccompanied, by yourself, on your own, single-handedly, unaided, without help, isolated and solitary.

Generally, people that like being alone don't like being in the company of other people because they prefer to be solitary. However, if you are in a relationship or married it's because you like being in sync with someone of the opposite sex. Therefore, since you like being jointly then you must once again do what jointly individual do and that is be as one, be together with your spouse or your significant other. In the following chapters we have put together a list of date night ideas, some of the ideas are for married couples only. We have also put together a list of date night ideas for couples in relationship. Don't give up so easy on your marriage or on a relationship that was once very good, they both can be very good once again. I think what people fail to realize is that marriage and a relationship both takes work and what you put into it is what you will get out of it. So from this day forward put God first in your marriage or relationship, make communication a vital and necessary part and what you sow you will surely reap.

3

Ideas for Married Couples Only

"Let thy fountain be blessed: and rejoice with the wife of thy youth." Proverbs 5:18

There are ideas and then there are ideas for married couples only. The reason there is a distinction between the two is because there are certain things that married couples can do according to the scriptures in the way of intimacy that couples only in a relationship cannot. Date night for married couples should end in physical intimacy or love making. Couples in relationship are warned to stay away from sex before marriage, the scripture calls it fornication. The word of the Lord is *"Flee fornication. Every sin that a man doeth is without the body; but he that committeth fornication sinneth against his own body. What? know ye not that your body is the temple of the Holy Ghost which is in you, which ye have of God, and ye are not your own? For ye are bought with a price: therefore glorify God in your body, and in your spirit, which are God's." 1 Corinthians 6:18-20*

Here are the Date Night Ideas for Married Couples Only along with other ideas that are just pertinent ideas for every couple.

1. Get a hotel room for your date night and order something in and have a night of great physical intimacy and love making. Let it be a mini-honeymoon night where you're starting all over again.

2. Take a bicycle ride for a good distance and then stop off and have a smoothie or some fruit drink.

3. Make tonight a date night where you will take a bubble bath together and light some candles and just relax.

4. Go to a movies together that both of you want to see and order a bucket of popcorn and one large soda with two straws.

5. Take a one night mini vacation where you can go in one day and return or on a weekend.

6. Go out to dinner tonight and have a nice dinner with just the two of you.

7. Have a candle light dinner with some non-alcoholic beverage that comes in the champagne bottle type and end the day with a card game of strip poker.

8. Watch a movie at home tonight and eat some popcorn and just enjoy each other.

9. Have a picnic on the inside and arrange everything just like you would be having one on the outside. Conclude the evening by taking a shower together.

10. Go out and order something and come back home to eat it together and just enjoy each other's company.

11. Serve your spouse dinner in bed make it a full event don't let her/him do a thing. Take a date night and do this for each other, make a date night his turn and then make one her turn.

12. Order a pizza tonight and just eat in and enjoy eating pizza and drinking your favorite beverages.

13. Cook a meal together for your date night that both of you will really enjoy.

14. Take a drive to your nearest beach and just enjoy a day at the beach with fun in the sun.

15. Go shopping together and treat each other, have a spending limit.

16. Set up a romantic dinner at a favorite restaurant where one of you has always being inquiring about and desiring to go.

17. Go with each other to get their hair done or get a haircut and then go out to dinner afterwards.

18. Be young again and go to McDonald's and enjoy a fast-food meal together inside.

19. Take a road trip together and enjoy the company of each other, stop by a nice eatery to get a good meal.

20. Go to a singles or marriage conference or retreat and learn something that can make your relationship or marriage better.

21. Spend time reading a good book together tonight and just enjoy each other's company. Make some sandwiches or something that doesn't take long to fix.

22. Go out to Star-bucks for your date night and enjoy a good cup of coffee or some other hot beverage and maybe a bagel.

23. Go out together and get a pedicure or manicure and enjoy this time of pampering the two of you.

24. Go to a special church service together which you have both being meaning to visit or partake of.

25. Go to a museum together and make it an educational night and afterwards go out and get something to eat.

26. Sign up for a class of some sort that both of you will enjoy and can do on your date night.

27. Visit an art gallery together and go out for brunch or lunch afterwards.

28. Let date night tonight be a night for games that you can play together and enjoy.

29. Cook something on the grill together and let this be a time of mutual bonding.

30. Do some fun activity together that both of you will enjoy such as bowling, golfing etc...

31. Go to poetry or author reading of a book that the both of you enjoy.

32. Check out an opera if the both of you are into that or just try it for a one time experience.

33. Take a walk in the park holding hands and stop to feed the birds. You can even plan a picnic for the evening.

34. Go to a play together and have a good laugh and just enjoy yourself.

35. Go to breakfast and then a matinee and enjoy an early movie together.

36. Take a one day cruise and make it a full day of excitement and pleasure.

37. Go check out a musical or concert which you both will enjoy as an event.

38. Go to a theme park and be kids again. Ride the rides and play some of the games.

39. Go to an outside restaurant like Sonics and enjoy dating and feeling young again.

40. Take a helicopter ride together and be adventurous then go out to lunch or dinner and laugh and talk about it.

41. Go out and take photos of different sceneries in your city and then go to lunch or dinner and look over them and discuss them.

42. Go out skating and afterwards sit in the skating rink and order something good to eat.

43. Go to an outdoor festival of some sort and spend the day there. Don't forget to try the large turkey legs.

44. Have an adventurous date night and try something wild like bungee jumping, sky diving, a balloon ride etc…

45. If you like the outdoors camp out if only in your back yard for the night.

46. Go to a live professional sporting event that you both will enjoy.

47. Build a web site together and enjoy a good snack while you're doing it.

48. Find a drive in movie and enjoy watching a movie in an old school way.

49. Arrange a date night where the two of you can sit in front of a fire and toast marshmallows and hotdogs.

50. Spend an hour together in prayer and fellowship with God. Afterwards go out to dinner and enjoy each other.

51. Go shopping together for things to make a date night meal where the both of you will cook together.

52. Go out moonlighting, where the two of you go out and sit under the moon and just enjoy each other.

53. Go to the circus together and enjoy a day of being like a kid again.

54. Take your partner and play a basketball game together for fun, a game of 21 or horse.

55. Take a day and go to the park and skateboard together.

56. Go to a game room and enjoy a good game of pool together and order some hot wings afterwards.

57. Challenge each other to a game of chess or checkers while eating chili cheese fries and drinking your favorite beverages.

58. Go hiking together and enjoy this time of challenging your partner.

59. Go hunting together during the time of hunting season and then come home and cook your catch.

60. Go fishing together and then cook the fish that you catch in the open fire.

61. Go to a bed and breakfast and allow someone else to wait on you both *hand and foot as the saying goes.*

62. Go to a batting cage and challenge each other to a game. Afterwards go out and get something to eat.

63. Go horseback riding and have a picnic afterwards.

64. Treat each other to an evening at a professional massage therapist.

65. Go out to your local book store and sit in for a couple of hours and just read together.

66. Rent a DVD of a movie that you both liked as a kid and just watch it together with popcorns and your favorite beverage, silly right, but it will be fun.

67. Take out the time to surprise your spouse or significant other and cook a foreign meal that the both of you like and dress up in that attire.

68. Sit in front of the fireplace and drink some hot tea, coffee etc… and just enjoy being together in your quite time.

69. Come together on a new hobby that the both of you can enjoy doing together.

70. For married couples, get a relative to keep the kids for the night and the two of you plan a festive night at home and be adventurous.

71. Set up a blind date with your spouse or significant other as if you have met up at the request of friends and go through the whole routine.

72. Go to a seminar together and learn something that the both of you have been itching to learn.

73. Go out and do something creative together such as build-a-bear or something similar and then go out to dinner afterward and take the bear of course.

74. Plan an event that the both of you can do together that will benefit others, such as doing a seminar about something both of you love to do.

75. Buy a recipe book and cook by recipe together something that you have never cooked before, be adventurous.

76. For married couples only, set the stage for a romantic night together, buy some new lingerie and some new perfume or cologne and spend a night of just making love over and over again.

77. Finally, whatever you do get back to old fashion dating ideas, like opening the car door when you go out, pull out the chair, open the door when you enter the restaurant and remember that the key word is doing something together. Oh yeah, why don't you take another couple out with you once and introduce them to date night.

4

Ideas for Couples in Relationship

"This is my beloved, and this is my friend, O daughters of Jerusalem." Song of Solomon 5:16

Here are ideas which couples in a relationship can enjoy. Couples in a relationship can use this time of their life to grow and bond together so that it will create a friendship during their relationship. Many couples in a relationship omit the time of friendship.

A friend is defined in Webster's dictionary as *one attached to another by respect or affection. One who supports or favors someone or something.* One of the missing ingredients in relationships today is friendship; many times individuals become lovers sexually even before they become friends. Not realizing that intimacy isn't going to make a person truly respect or become affectionate toward them, nor will it cause an individual to support or favor them. The scriptures have many things to say concerning a friend that will enlighten you in your understanding of how it relates to relationships when you have found a true friend.

1. *A friend loveth at all times. Proverbs 17:17*

2. *A man that hath friends must shew himself friendly: and there is a friend that sticketh closer than a brother. Proverbs 18:24*

3. *Faithful are the wounds of a friend. Proverbs 27:6*

4. *Ointment and perfume rejoice the heart: so doth the sweetness of a man's friend by hearty counsel. Proverbs 27:9 35*

5. *Greater love hath no man than this, that a man lay down his life for his friends. Ye are my friends, if ye do whatsoever I command you. Henceforth I call you not servants; for the servant knoweth not what his lord doeth: but I have called you friends; for all things that I have heard of my Father I have made known unto you. John 15:13-15*

If you fail to become friends before you become seriously involved with one another you will not be in a relationship with someone that will love you at all times, but will only love you conditionally. In order for the two of you to become friends with each other you both must first show yourself friendly towards each other in words, deed and in truth. For if you can't show yourself friendly then you will not have an individual in your corner that will stick with you through thick and thin, good and bad, richer or poorer and till death do you part. If you have only encountered dates, the one thing that has been void in your relationships is true and lasting friendship. A true friend will not only tell you the truth even if it hurts, but will also bring you pleasantness and hearty counsel and good advice when needed. A true friend because they are true will not demand that things always be their way, but will be willing to lay down their life (or manner of thinking and doing) in order to keep harmony and peace in the friendship.

A true friend will not keep things away from you, but will be willing to disclose and expose themselves to you knowing that they can do this in confidence for you are their friend. Jesus said *"Henceforth I call you not servants; for the servant knoweth not what his lord doeth: but I have called you friends; for all things I have heard of my Father I have made known unto you." John* 15:15 True friendship takes time, love can happen quickly, but true love grows and develops as it gives space for friendship to mature it and make it fruitful. When true love is enveloped in true friendship then you have encountered a relationship that can only be described according to love exemplified in the scriptures:

- *Love suffereth long, and is kind;*
- *Love envieth not;*
- *Love vaunteth not itself, is not puffed up;.*
- *Love doth not behave itself unseemly;*

- *Love seeketh not her own, is not easily provoked and thinketh no evil;*
- *Love rejoiceth not in iniquity, but rejoiceth in the truth;*
- *Love beareth all things, believeth all things, hopeth all things, endureth all things.*
- *Love never fails. 1 Corinthians 13: 4-8a*

True friendship will respect one another's morals and decisions, it will not ask one to do wrong when the other has stipulated boundaries and beliefs. Let me give you an example: If you're in a relationship with someone and you tell them that because of your Christian belief and relationship with Christ you don't desire to engage in sex outside of marriage or any sexual activities, a true friend will respect this.

An individual that's not a true friend will try to persuade you with many reasons and excuses why the two of you should engage in sex or sexual activities even though they know how you feel about the situation. Remember, the definition of friend according to Webster is *one attached to another by respect or affection. One who supports or favors someone or* something.

You don't want excuses, reasons or persuasions from one that is supposed to be your friend, you want respect, affection, support and favor and this you will get from a true friend and this is the type of person that can be your soul mate. When you find this type of friend you will find your ***rayah*** (Strong's Concordance ref 7453), this is the Hebrew word in scripture that is defined as companion, friend, husband, wife ***and lover.*** In your endeavor to find and be found of your soul mate don't settle for less than your rayah, for in your rayah you will find *a friend that loves at all times, a friend that sticks closer than a brother and a friend that will lay down their life for you.* With this person you will enjoy a celebration of love that comes when you have found your soul mate and not just another date. Here are date night ideas for couples in relationship.

1. Take a bicycle ride for a good distance and then stop off and have a smoothie or some fruit drink.

2. Go to a movies together that both of you want to see and order the bucket of popcorn and one large soda with two straws.

3. Take a one day mini vacation where you can go in one day and return.

4. Go out to dinner tonight and have a nice dinner with just the two of you.

5. Have a candle light dinner with some non-alcoholic beverage that comes in the champagne bottle type.

6. Watch a movie at home tonight and eat some popcorn and just enjoy each other.

7. Go out moonlighting, where the two of you go out and sit under the moon and just enjoy each other.

8. Have a picnic on the inside and arrange everything just like you would be having one on the outside.

9. Go out and order something and come back home to eat it together and just enjoy each other company.

10. Order a pizza tonight and just eat in and enjoy eating pizza and drinking your favorite beverages.

11. Cook a meal together for your date night that both of you will really enjoy

12. Take a drive to your nearest beach and just enjoy a day at the beach with fun in the sun.

13. Go shopping together and treat each other, have a spending limit.

14. Set up a romantic dinner at a favorite restaurant where one of you have always being inquiring about and wanting to go.

15. Go with each other to get their hair done or get a haircut and then go out to dinner afterwards.

16. Be young again and go to McDonald's and enjoy a fast-food meal together inside.

17. Take a road trip together and enjoy the company of each other, stop by a nice eatery to get a good meal.

18. Go to a singles or marriage conference or retreat and learn something that can make your relationship or marriage better.

19. Spend time reading a good book together tonight and just enjoy each other's company. Make some sandwiches or something that doesn't take long to fix.

20. Go out to Star-bucks for your date night and enjoy a good cup of coffee or some other hot beverage and maybe a bagel.

21. Go out together and get a pedicure or manicure and enjoy this time of pampering the two of you.

22. Go to a special church service together which you have both being meaning to visit or partake of.

23. Go to a museum together and make it an educational night and afterwards go out and get something to eat.

24. Sign up for a class of some sort that both of you will enjoy and cake take on your date night.

25. Visit an art gallery together and go out for brunch or lunch afterwards.

26. Let date night tonight be a night for games that you can play together and enjoy.

27. Cook something on the grill together and let this be a time of mutual bonding.

28. Do some fun activity together that both of you will enjoy such as bowling, golfing etc…

29. Go to poetry or author reading of a book that the both of you enjoy.

30. Check out an opera if the both of you are into that or just try it for a one time experience.

31. Talk a walk in the park holding hands and stop to feed the birds. You can even plan a picnic for the evening.

32. Go to a play together and have a good laugh and just enjoy yourself.

33. Go to breakfast and then a matinee and enjoy an early movie together.

34. Take a one day cruise and make it a full day of excitement and pleasure.

35. Go check out a musical or concert which you both will enjoy as an event.

36. Go to a theme park and be kids again. Ride the rides and play some of the games.

37. Go to an outside restaurant like Sonics and enjoy dating and feeling young again.

38. Take a helicopter ride together and be adventurous then go out to lunch or dinner and laugh and talk about it.

39. Go out and take photos of different sceneries in your city and then go to lunch or dinner and look over them and discuss them.

40. Go out skating and afterwards sit in the skating rink and order something good to eat.

41. Go to an outdoor festival of some sort and spend the day there. Don't forget to try the large turkey legs.

42. Have an adventurous date night and try something wild like bungee jumping, sky diving, a balloon ride etc…

43. If you like the outdoors camp out if only in your back yard for the night.

44. Go to a live professional sporting event that you both will enjoy.

45. Build a web site together and enjoy a good snack while you're doing it.

46. Find a drive in move and enjoy watching a movie in an old school way.

47. Arrange a date night where the two of you can sit in front of a fire and toast marshmallows and hotdogs.

48. Spend an hour together in prayer and fellowship with God. Afterwards go out to dinner and enjoy each other.

49. Go shopping together for things to make a date night meal where the both of you will cook together.

50. Go to the circus together and enjoy a day of being like a kid again.

51. Take your partner and play a basketball game together for fun, a game of 21 or horse.

52. Take a day and go to the park and skateboard together.

53. Go to a game room and enjoy a good game of pool together and order some hot wings afterwards.

54. Challenge each other to a game of chess or checkers while eating chili cheese fries and drinking your favorite beverages.

55. Go hiking together and enjoy this time of challenging your partner.

56. Go hunting together during the time of hunting season and then come home and cook your catch.

57. Go fishing together and then cook the fish that you catch in the open fire.

58. Go to a batting cage and challenge each other to a game. Afterwards go out and get something to eat.

59. Go horseback riding and have a picnic afterwards.

60. Treat each other to an evening at a professional massage therapist.

61. Go out to your local book store and sit in for a couple of hours and just read together.

62. Rent a DVD of a movie that you both liked as a kid and just watch it together with popcorns and your favorite beverage, silly right, but it will be fun.

63. Take out the time to surprise your spouse or significant other and cook a foreign meal that the both of you like and dress up in that attire.

64. Sit in front of the fireplace and drink some hot tea, coffee etc… and just enjoy being together in your quite time.

65. Come together on a new hobby that the both of you can enjoy doing together.

66. Set up a blind date with your significant other as if you have met up at the request of friends and go through the whole routine.

67. Go to a seminar together and learn something that the both of you have been itching to learn.

68. Go out and do something creative together such as build-a-bear or something similar and then go out to dinner afterward and take the bear of course.

69. Plan an event that the both of you can do together that will benefit others, such as doing a seminar about something both of you love to do.

70. Buy a recipe book and cook by recipe together something that you have never cooked before, be adventurous.

71. Have a dress up night and go out to dinner or too a movie, dressed in a costume of some sort, silly yes, but it will be fun.

72. If you live near a drive-in theater or not to far from one, let this be a date night idea, it will blow your mind. In a good way!

73. Go out window shopping and look at the things that you will buy for each other for an upcoming occasion and then go out to lunch.

74. Set up your own comedy club night where the two of you become comedians for the night, one of you will be the audience for the other. Enjoy laughing together with each other.

75. Take out time to go and volunteer together doing something for someone else…serving at the shelter, feeding the homeless or visiting the elderly at rest homes.

76. Go to a flea market together and walk around eating and enjoying all the vendors and what they're selling. Don't forget to buy something from them also.

77. Finally, whatever you do get back to old fashion dating ideas, like opening the car door when you go out, pull out the chair, open the door when you enter the restaurant and remember that the key word is doing something together. Oh yeah, why don't you take another couple out with you once and introduce them to date night.

5

God's Ideal Relationship

My beloved spake, and said unto me, Rise up, my love, my fair one, and come away." Song of Solomon 2:10

The closest idea we have of a harmonious and compatible relationship of two people in love is exemplified in the scriptures according to the Song of Solomon. Here we have two people that are obviously soul mates. The communication and attraction between these two people displays love of the highest order; it shows respect, consideration, passion, compassion, kindness, unselfishness, patience, temperance, faith, hope and belief. Notice the terminology which they use and the easy display of verbal affection to one another, the honesty, sincerity and excitement of just being in one another's presence. We don't attempt to interpret the words of these two individuals that are wonderfully in love. We just give it to you as it is and allow the Holy Spirit to enlighten your mind and speak to your spirit as you read it. Notice the love and beauty of it all as we listen to two people that are immensely in love with one another as it should be. Listen as the emotions run high and the feelings of each are spoken effortlessly. There is no holding back here because each desires the other to know what they think and how they feel. Read it slowly and observe the words they're speaking.

Let us now behold "The song of songs, which is Solomon's. Let him kiss me with the kisses of his mouth: for thy love is better than wine. Because of the savour of thy good ointments thy name is as ointment poured forth, therefore do the virgins love thee. Draw me, we will run after thee: the king hath brought me into his chambers: we will be glad and rejoice in thee, we will remember thy love more than wine: the upright love thee. I am black, but comely, O ye daughters of Jerusalem, as the tents of Kedar, as the curtains of Solomon. Look not upon me, because I am black, because the sun hath looked upon me: my mother's children were angry with me; they made me the keeper of the vineyards; but mine own vineyard have I not kept.

Tell me, O thou whom my soul loveth, where thou feedest, where thou makest thy flock to rest at noon: for why should I be as one that turneth aside by the flocks of thy companions? If thou know not, O thou fairest among women, go thy way forth by the footsteps of the flock, and feed thy kids beside the shepherds' tents. I have compared thee, O my love, to a company of horses in Pharaoh's chariots. Thy cheeks are comely with rows of jewels, thy neck with chains of gold. We will make thee borders of gold with studs of silver. While the king sitteth at his table, my spikenard sendeth forth the smell thereof. A bundle of myrrh is my well-beloved unto me; he shall lie all night betwixt my breasts.

My beloved is unto me as a cluster of camphire in the vineyards of En-gedi. Behold, thou art fair, my love; behold, thou art fair; thou hast doves' eyes. Behold, thou art fair, my beloved, yea, pleasant: also our bed is green. The beams of our house are cedar, and our rafters of fir. I am the rose of Sharon, and the lily of the valleys. As the lily among thorns, so is my love among the daughters. As the apple tree among the trees of the wood, so is my beloved among the sons. I sat down under his shadow with great delight, and his fruit was sweet to my taste. He brought me to the banqueting house, and his banner over me was love. Stay me with flagons, comfort me with apples: for I am sick of love. His left hand is under my head, and his right hand doth embrace me. I charge you, O ye daughters of Jerusalem, by the roes, and by the hinds of the field, that ye stir not up, nor awake my love, till he please.

The voice of my beloved! behold, he cometh leaping upon the mountains, skipping upon the hills. My beloved is like a roe or a young hart: behold, he standeth behind our wall, he looketh forth at the windows, shewing himself through the lattice. My beloved spake, and said unto me, Rise up, my love, my fair one, and come away. For, lo, the winter is past, the rain is over and gone; The flowers appear on the earth; the time of the singing of birds is come, and the voice of the turtle is heard in our land;

The fig tree putteth forth her green figs, and the vines with the tender grape give a good smell. Arise, my love, my fair one, and come away. O my dove, that art in the clefts of the rock, in the secret places of the stairs, let me see thy countenance, let me hear thy voice; for sweet is thy voice, and thy countenance is comely.

Take us the foxes, the little foxes, that spoil the vines: for our vines have tender grapes. My beloved is mine, and I am his: he feedth among the lilies. Until the day break, and the shadows flee away, turn, my beloved, and be thou like a roe or a young hart upon the mountains of Bether. By night on my bed I sought him whom my soul loveth: I sought him, but I found him not. I will rise now, and go about the city in the streets, and in the broad ways I will seek him whom my soul loveth: I sought him, but I found him not. The watchmen that go about the city found me: to whom I said, Saw ye him whom my soul loveth? It was but a little that I passed from them, but I found him whom my soul loveth: I held him, and would not let him go, until I had brought him into my mother's house, and into the chamber of her that conceived me. I charge you, O ye daughters of Jerusalem, by the roes, and by the hinds of the field, that ye stir not up, nor awake my love, till he please. Who is this that cometh out of the wilderness like pillars of smoke, perfumed with myrrh and frankincense, with all powders of the merchant?

Behold his bed, which is Solomon's; threescore valiant men are about it, of the valiant of Israel. They all hold swords, being expert in war: every man hath his sword upon his thigh because of fear in the night. King Solomon made himself a chariot of the wood of Lebanon. He made pillars thereof of silver, the bottom thereof of gold, the covering of it of purple, the midst thereof being paved with love, for the daughters of Jerusalem. Go forth, O ye daughters of Zion, and behold king Solomon with the crown wherewith his mother crowned him in the day of his espousals, and in the day of the gladness of his heart. Behold, thou art fair, my love; behold, thou art fair; thou hast doves' eyes within thy locks: thy hair is as a flock of goats, that appear from mount Gilead. Thy teeth are like a flock of sheep that are even shorn, which came up from the washing; whereof every one bear twins, and none is barren among them. Thy lips are like a thread of scarlet, and thy speech is comely: thy temples are like a piece of a pomegranate within thy locks. Thy neck is like the tower of David builded for an armoury, whereon there hang a thousand bucklers, all shields of mighty men. Thy two breasts are like two young roes that are twins, which feed among the lilies. Until the day break, and the shadows flee away, I will get me to the mountain of myrrh, and to the hill of frankincense. Thou art all fair, my love; there is no spot in thee. Come with me from Lebanon, my spouse, with me from Lebanon: look from the top of Amana, from the top of Shenir and Hermon, from the lions' dens, from the mountains of the leopards. Thou hast ravished my heart, my sister, my spouse; thou hast ravished my heart with one of thine eyes, with one chain of thy neck. How fair is thy love, my sister, my spouse! How much better is thy love than wine! and the smell of thine ointments than all spices! Thy lips, O my spouse, drop as the honeycomb: honey and milk are under thy tongue; and the smell of thy garments is like the smell of Lebanon. A garden inclosed is my sister, my spouse; a spring shut up, a fountain sealed.

Thy plants are an orchard of pomegranates, with pleasant fruits; camphire, with spikenard, Spikenard and saffron; calamus and cinnamon, with all trees of frankincense; myrrh and aloes, with all the chief spices: A fountain of gardens, a well of living waters, and streams from Lebanon. Awake, O north wind; and come, thou south; blow upon my garden, that the spices thereof may flow out. Let my beloved come into his garden and eat his pleasant fruits. I am come into my garden, my sister, my spouse: I have gathered my myrrh with my spice; I have eaten my honeycomb with my honey; I have drunk my wine with my milk: eat, O friends; drink, yea, drink abundantly, O beloved. I sleep, but my heart waketh: it is the voice of my beloved that knocketh, saying, Open to me, my sister, my love, my dove, my undefiled: for my head is filled with dew, and my locks with the drops of the night.

I have put off my coat; how shall I put it on? I have washed my feet; how shall I defile them? My beloved put in his hand by the hole of the door, and my bowels were moved for him. I rose up to open to my beloved; and my hand dropped with myrrh, and my fingers with sweet smelling myrrh, upon the handles of the lock. I opened to my beloved; but my beloved had withdrawn himself, and was gone: my soul failed when he spake: I sought him, but I could not find him; I called him, but he gave me no answer. The watchmen that went about the city found me, they smote me, they wounded me; the keepers of the walls took away my veil from me. I charge you, O daughter of Jerusalem, if ye find my beloved, that ye tell him, that I am sick of love.

What is thy beloved more than another beloved, O thou fairest among women? what is thy beloved more than another beloved, that thou dost so charge us? My beloved is white and ruddy, the chiefest among ten thousand. His head is as the most fine gold, his locks are bushy, and black as a raven. His eyes are as the eyes of doves by the rivers of water, washed with milk, and fitly set. His cheeks are as a bed of spices, as sweet flowers: his lips like lilies, dropping sweet smelling myrrh. His hands are as gold rings set with the beryl: his belly is as bright ivory overlaid with sapphires. His legs are as pillars of marble, set upon sockets of fine gold: his countenance is as Lebanon, excellent as the cedars

His mouth is most sweet: yea, he is altogether lovely. This is my beloved, and this is my friend, O daughters of Jerusalem. Whither is thy beloved gone, O thou fairest among women? whither is thy beloved turned aside? that we may seek him with thee. My beloved is gone down into his garden, to the bed of spices, to feed in the gardens, and to gather lilies. I am my beloved's, and my beloved is mine: he feedeth among the lilies. Thou art beautiful, O my love, as Tirzah, comely as Jerusalem, terrible as an army with banners. Turn away thine eyes from me, for they have overcome me: thy hair is as a flock of goats that appear from Gilead. Thy teeth are as a flock of sheep which go up from the washing, whereof every one beareth twins, and there is not one barren among them. As a piece of a pomegranate are thy temples within thy locks. There are threescore queens, and fourscore concubines, and virgins without number.

My dove, my undefiled is but one; she is the only one of her mother, she is the choice one of her that bare her. The daughters saw her, and blessed her; yea, the queens and the concubines, and they praised her. Who is she that looketh forth as the morning, fair as the moon, clear as the sun, and terrible as an army with banners? I went down into the garden of nuts to see the fruits of the valley, and to see whether the vine flourished, and the pomegranates budded. Or ever I was aware, my soul made me like the chariots of Ammi-nadib.

Return, return, O Shulamite; return, return, that we may look upon thee. What will ye see in the Shulamite? As it were the company of two armies. How beautiful are thy feet with shoes, O prince's daughter! the joints of thy thighs are like jewels, the work of the hands of a cunning workman. Thy navel is like a round goblet, which wanteth not liquor: thy belly is like an heap of wheat set about with lilies.

Thy two breasts are like two young roes that are twins. Thy neck is as a tower of ivory: thine eyes like the fishpools in Heshbon, by the gate of Bathrabbim: thy nose is as the tower of Lebanon which looketh toward Damascus. Thine head upon thee is like Carmel, and the hair of thine head like purple; the king is held in the galleries. How fair and how pleasant art thou, O love, for delights! This thy stature is like to a palm tree, and thy breasts to clusters of grapes. I said, I will go up to the palm tree, I will take hold of the boughs thereof: now also thy breasts shall be as the clusters of the vine, and the smell of thy nose like apples; And the roof of thy mouth like the best wine for my beloved, that goeth down sweetly, causing the lips of those that are asleep to speak.

I am my beloved's, and his desire is toward me. Come, my beloved, let us go forth into the field; let us lodge in the villages. Let us get up early to the vineyards; let us see if the vine flourish, whether the tender grape appear, and the pomegranates bud forth: there will I give thee my love. The mandrakes give a smell, and at our gates are all manner of pleasant fruits, new and old, which I have laid up for thee, O my beloved. O that thou wert as my brother, that sucked the breasts of my mother! when I should find thee without, I would kiss thee; yea, I should not be despised. I would lead thee, and bring thee into my mother's house, who would instruct me: I would cause thee to drink of spiced wine of the juice of my pomegranate.

His left hand should be under my head, and his right hand should embrace me. I charge you, O daughters of Jerusalem, that ye stir not up, nor awake my love, until he pleased. Who is this that cometh up from the wilderness, leaning upon her beloved? I raised thee up under the apple tree: there thy mother brought thee forth: there she brought thee forth that bare thee. Set me as a seal upon thine heart, as a seal upon thine arm: for love is strong as death; jealousy is cruel as the grave: the coals thereof are coals of fire, which hath a most vehement flame. Many waters cannot quench love, neither can the floods drown it: if a man would give all the substance of his house for love, it would be utterly contemned.

We have a little sister, and she hath no breasts: what shall we do for our sister in the day when she shall be spoken for? If she be a wall, we will build upon her a palace of silver:

and if she be a door, we will inclose her with boards of cedar. I am a wall, and my breasts like towers; then was I in his eyes as one that found favour. Solomon had a vineyard at Baal-hamon; he let out the vineyard unto keepers; everyone for the fruit thereof was to bring a thousand pieces of silver. My vineyard, which is mine, is before me: thou, O Solomon, must have a thousand, and those that keep the fruit thereof two hundred. Thou that dwellest in the gardens, the companions hearken to thy voice: cause me to hear it. Make hast, my beloved, and be thou like to a roe or to a young hart upon the mountain of spices." Song of Solomon 1-8

6

Walk In Love

"I therefore, the prisoner of the Lord, beseech you that ye walk worthy of the vocation wherewith ye are called. With all lowliness and meekness, with longsuffering, forbearing one another in love; Endeavoring to keep the unity of the Spirit in the bond of peace." Ephesians 4:1-3

What better way to end this book than a chapter that speaks on walking in love for love is the fulfilling of every law? As people of God we should be loving people and exemplify the love of God in our lives, for the scripture says; *"because the love of God is shed abroad in our hearts by the Holy Ghost which is given unto us." Romans 5:5* Take the love test and see if you're walking in love according to the scriptures and if not *"let love be"* for love is in you desiring to come out of you and be shed abroad upon others. Love is the greatest of all and no matter what else you may have or do, without love you're building a foundation upon sand. Jesus said *"And every one that heareth these sayings of mine, and doeth them not, shall be likened unto a foolish man, which built his house upon the sand: And the rain descended, and the floods came, and the winds blew, and beat upon that house; and it fell: and great was the fall of it." Matthew 7:26-27*

THE GREATEST OF THESE IS LOVE

"Though I speak with the tongues of men and of angels, and have not charity (love), I am become as sounding brass, or a tinkling cymbal. And though I have the gift of prophecy, and understand all mysteries, and all knowledge; and though I have all faith, so that I could remove mountains, and have not charity (love), I am nothing. And though I bestow all my goods to feed the poor, and though I give my body to be burned, and have not charity (love), it profiteth me nothing.

Charity suffereth long, and is kind; charity envieth not; charity vaunteth not itself, is not puffed up, Doth not behave itself unseemly, seeketh not her own, is not easily provoked, thinketh no evil; Rejoiceth not in iniquity, but rejoiceth in the truth; Beareth all things, believeth all things, hopeth all things, endureth all things. Charity never faileth: but whether there be prophecies, they shall fail; whether there be tongues, they shall cease; whether there be knowledge, it shall vanish away. For we know in part, and we prophesy in part. But when that which is perfect is come, then that which is in part shall be done away. When I was a child, I spake as a child, I understood as a child, I thought as a child: but when I became a man, I put away childish things. For now we see through a glass, darkly' but then face to face:

now I know in part; but then shall I know even as also I am known. And now abideth faith, hope, charity, these three; but the greatest of these is charity." 1 Corinthians 13

The Greatest Relationship of All

As God's servant I could not with all good conscience end this book without offering you the opportunity to experience the greatest relationship of all. All other relationships pale in comparison to establishing a relationship with your creator and maker; *"For he hath made him to be sin for us, who knew no sin; that we might be made the righteousness of God in him. He that spared not his own Son, but delivered him up for us all, how shall he not with him also freely give us all things?" 2 Corinthians 5:21, Romans 8:32*

God wants a relationship with you and he gave his Son who gave his life for you and me to reconcile us to God. *"For when we were yet without strength, in due time Christ died for the ungodly. For scarcely for a righteous man will one die: yet peradventure for a good man some would even dare to die. But God commendeth his love toward us, in that, while we were yet sinners, Christ died for us." Romans 5:6-8*

You can receive Jesus Christ into your life right now as your Lord and Savior and receive eternal life.

It's simple really, you just ask Jesus to come into your life with this simple prayer:

"Dear God, according to your word I have sinned and come short of the glory of God. I stand in need of the Savior Jesus Christ. I repent of my sins and ask Jesus to come into my life. I acknowledge that I am a sinner and need to be saved. I believe that Jesus died, was buried and was resurrected and is now alive at your right hand. I ask that the blood of Jesus cleanse me from all sins and I accept Jesus into my life now. Father, I thank you for receiving me, I am now a child of God, I'm saved and my name is written in the lambs book of life, in Jesus name. Amen"

Tell us about your decision in receiving Jesus Christ as your Lord and Savior, we will get you out some literature as soon as possible, God bless you and keep you.

You can also email us at:
soulmateorjustadate@yahoo.com
or visit our web site at
www.soulmateorjustadate.com

Check out our other websites at:
www.firstclasswebsite.com
www.uwriteitpublishingcompany.com
www.aoccsingles-ministry.socialgo.com

www.ingramcontent.com/pod-product-compliance
Lightning Source LLC
Chambersburg PA
CBHW061514040426
42450CB00008B/1612